POWER ENGLISH

BASIC LANGUAGE SKILLS FOR ADULTS

Dorothy Rubin

TRENTON STATE COLLEGE

GLOBE FEARON EDUCATIONAL PUBLISHER
Upper Saddle River, New Jersey
www.globefearon.com

Editorial supervision: Timothy Foote
Production supervision: Alan Gold
Manufacturing buyer: Mike Woerner

Printed in the United States of America

10   9   8   7

ISBN 0-13-688441-5

PRENTICE-HALL INTERNATIONAL (UK) LIMITED, LONDON
PRENTICE-HALL OF AUSTRALIA PTY. LIMITED, SYDNEY
PRENTICE-HALL CANADA INC., TORONTO
PRENTICE-HALL HISPANOAMERICANA, S.A., MEXICO
PRENTICE-HALL OF INDIA PRIVATE LIMITED, NEW DELHI
PRENTICE-HALL OF JAPAN, INC., TOKYO
PEARSON EDUCATION ASIA PTE. LTD., SINGAPORE
EDITORA PRENTICE-HALL DO BRASIL, LTDA., RIO DE JANEIRO

CONTENTS

CHAPTER THREE

CHAPTER FOUR   63

TO THE TEACHER

Power English: Basic Language Skills for Adults is a ten-book series dedicated to helping adults at the ABE level develop their skills in usage, sentence structure, mechanics, and composition. *Power English* consists of the locator test for the series, eight text/workbooks, and a series review book.

There are five chapters in each of the text/workbooks. The several lessons in each chapter cover a variety of writing skills. The comprehensive Chapter Reviews and Posttests in each book provide skill reinforcement. To facilitate diagnosis, there are Progress Charts for recording students' Chapter Review and Posttest performance. Answers are in a special section at the end of each book. The section can be left in the book so that students can check their own work, or since its pages are perforated, it can be removed.

Power English is comfortable for an adult whose reading level is between 4.0 and 8.0. Each lesson is a simple and concise presentation of a specific writing skill. In the instructional portion of a lesson, under the heading **Read the following** students study examples of a specific writing skill at work. Under **Did you notice?** they read short, clear explanations of the skill at hand. Because a typical lesson reinforces and expands upon skills taught in earlier lessons, a section called **Do you remember?** reviews pertinent rules and concepts previously presented. The

Try it out portion of a lesson provides exercise for applying and practicing the new and reviewed skills.

Power English encourages the rapid and enjoyable acquisition of fundamental writing skills. The program is based on sound learning principles and is devised to keep the student actively engaged throughout. It incorporates the following:

- self-pacing
- graduated levels of difficulty
- distributed practice
- immediate feedback
- overlearning
- teaching of generalizations where applicable
- selections based on adult interests

Power English is founded on the principle of overlearning, which fosters enduring retention of information and skills. Overlearning occurs when students continue practicing a skill even after they think they have learned it. In every chapter and book in the *Power English* series, through a variety of formats, students exercise skills they have learned in previous chapters and books.

The structure of the *Power English* series makes it versatile. It can be used in conventional classroom settings, in tutorial situations and clinics, or by students who work independently.

POWER ENGLISH

CHAPTER ONE

CAPITAL LETTERS

Read the following:

A B C D E F G H I J K L M N O P Q R S T U V W X Y Z
a b c d e f g h i j k l m n o p q r s t u v w x y z

Now read the following:

George Brown	Ling Huang
Barbara Crandall	José Melendez
Henri Duval	Nat Turner

Did you notice?

The letters in the first row are all capital letters.
The letters in the second row are all small letters.
People's names begin with capital letters.

Try it out.

Write these names over. Use capital letters correctly.

1. george washington _____

2. barry grant _____

3. paolo russo _____

4. monique martin _____

5. harvey green _____

6. marie veldez _____

7. hiro sato _____

8. ali yussef _____

9. abraham levine _____

10. carla florino _____

STOP CHECK ANSWERS ON PAGE 119.

CAPITAL LETTERS

Try it out.

Write these sentences over. Use capital letters correctly.

1. my friend ricardo and his girlfriend are getting married soon.

_____

2. i only see ricardo at work now.

_____

3. he spends all his time with maria.

_____

4. my brother dave and i are planning a party for him.

_____

5. my sister sara is planning a party for maria.

_____

STOP CHECK ANSWERS ON PAGE 119.

TELLING SENTENCES (STATEMENTS)

Read the following:

Mike and Julia both work.
They want to earn more money.
They want to move.
Julia is expecting a baby.

Did you notice?

Each sentence tells something.

Did you know?

Sentences that tell something are called **statements**.
A telling sentence ends with a period (.).

Do you remember?

Sentences and people's names begin with capital letters.

Try it out.

Write the following telling sentences over. Use correct capital letters and end marks.

1. i have worked with mike for five years

   _____

2. he is my best friend

   _____

3. we go everywhere together

   _____

4. last year we went on a camping trip

   _____

5. julia and my wife are also good friends

   _____

GO ON TO THE NEXT PAGE

6. they go shopping together all the time

_____

7. i would miss mike if he moved away

_____

8. my wife would miss julia

_____

9. mike and julia need money to take care of the new baby

_____

10. they could make more money in another city

_____

STOP CHECK ANSWERS ON PAGE 119.

ASKING SENTENCES (QUESTIONS)

Read the following:

Who is there?
What do you want?
When do you want your lunch?
Where should I catch the bus?
Why should I go?

How much will you pay me?
Is Florence home?
Are the children at school?
Do you like old movies?
Have you seen this movie?

Did you notice?

Each sentence asks a question.
An asking sentence ends with a question mark (?).

Did you know?

Many questions begin with these words:
Who   What   When   Where   Why   How
Other questions begin with words such as these:
Is   Are   Do   Have

Do you remember?

Sentences and people's names begin with capital letters.

Try it out.

Write the following questions over. Use correct capital letters and end marks.

1. how old is florence

   _____

2. when are we going there

   _____

3. is florence always so nice

   _____

4. who told you those lies

   _____

5. do you want to know the truth

   _____

STOP CHECK ANSWERS ON PAGE 119.

END MARKS

Read the following:

Seth loves to read.
Carmen loves to write letters.

Now read the following:

Who loves to read?
What does Carmen love to do?

Do you remember?

Telling sentences, or statements, end with a period (.).
Asking sentences, or questions, end with a question mark (?).

Try it out.

Put the correct end mark at the end of each sentence.

1. Monique is going back to school

2. How old is she

3. She is 24 years old

4. Why is she going back to school

5. Is she unhappy with her job

6. Did she get fired

7. Monique wants to get a better job

8. Does she have the time to go back to school

9. Will her husband help her

10. Her husband is glad she is going back to school

STOP CHECK ANSWERS ON PAGE 119.

NAMING WORDS (NOUNS)

Read the following:

child	bird	bus	city	fear
husband	cat	hand	farm	happiness
mother	dog	house	town	health

Did you notice?

Each of the words names something.
The words name persons, animals, things, places, ideas, or feelings.
All the words are naming words, or **nouns**.

Now read the following:

The naming words, or nouns, are underlined in these sentences:
The <u>worker</u> left the <u>factory</u>.
Please give my <u>regards</u> to your <u>mother</u>.
Her <u>horse</u> won the <u>prize</u>.

Try it out.

Fill in each blank with a noun from this list. Use each noun **only once**. Be sure the completed sentences make sense.

NOUN LIST

boss	child	house	~~job~~	laborer
money	school	student	teacher	yard

1. Jim has a good _____.

2. His _____ is a hard person to please.

3. Jim is a _____.

4. Jim has a wife and a _____.

5. She also works long hours to earn _____.

6. They want to buy a _____.

7. They want a big _____.

8. Jim goes to _____ at night.

9. Jim is a good _____ in class.

10. His _____ is helping him learn to write better.

STOP CHECK ANSWERS ON PAGE 119.

RECOGNIZING NAMING WORDS (NOUNS)

Read the following:

My <u>wife</u> jogs regularly.
Her <u>health</u> is very good.

Did you notice?

There is one naming word, or noun, in each sentence.
The nouns are underlined.

Try it out.

Draw a line under the noun in each sentence.

1. My wife wants to move.

2. Her family lives here.

3. That garden is beautiful.

4. Our house is very old.

5. This room is very small.

6. There was a small fire here.

7. The dog was frightened.

8. The street needs to be cleaned.

9. That car went by too fast.

10. My block is dangerous.

STOP CHECK ANSWERS ON PAGE 119.

MORE THAN ONE (PLURAL)

Read the following:

one <u>worker</u>	five <u>workers</u>
a <u>dog</u>	all <u>dogs</u>
the <u>rock</u>	several <u>rocks</u>
a <u>street</u>	both <u>streets</u>
a <u>hope</u>	their <u>hopes</u>
my <u>pain</u>	my <u>pains</u>

Did you notice?

The nouns in the lists are underlined.
Some nouns name one person, animal, thing, place, idea, or feeling.
Other nouns name more than one person, animal, thing, place, idea, or feeling.
Many nouns that name more than one end with an **s**.

Did you know?

Singular nouns name one person, animal, thing, place, idea, or feeling.
Plural nouns name more than one.

Try it out.

Add an **s** to any noun that names more than one person, animal, thing, place, idea, or feeling.

1. a brother	6. a bank	11. all lamp	16. five month
2. five sister	7. some bag	12. ten grape	17. some dog
3. both girl	8. a tree	13. a joy	18. two pet
4. four apple	9. several job	14. nine year	19. a thought
5. one desk	10. a clock	15. a town	20. both name

STOP CHECK ANSWERS ON PAGE 119.

MORE THAN ONE (PLURAL)

Read the following:

a <u>kiss</u>	some <u>kisses</u>
one <u>class</u>	two <u>classes</u>
a <u>glass</u>	both <u>glasses</u>
one <u>bus</u>	four <u>buses</u>

Did you notice?

The nouns in the lists are underlined.
Some singular nouns end with **s** or **ss**.
Those nouns end with **es** when they are plural.

Do you remember?

Singular nouns name one person, animal, thing, place, idea, or feeling.
Plural nouns name more than one.
Many nouns that name more than one end with an **s**: workers, dogs, rocks, streets.

Try it out.

Add an **s** or **es** ending to any noun that needs one.

1. one apple
2. three dress
3. a mess
4. some tree
5. five pass
6. two boss
7. several bird
8. five bug
9. two row
10. both princess

STOP CHECK ANSWERS ON PAGE 119.

ACTION WORDS (VERBS)

Read the following:

The train <u>runs</u> fast.
My girlfriend <u>works</u>.
Her cat <u>chases</u> mice.
This dog <u>barks</u> at cars.

Did you notice?

In each sentence a word is underlined.
Those words are action words, or **verbs**.

Did you know?

Verbs give part of the meaning to sentences.
Verbs let you know what actions sentences tell about.

Try it out.

Fill in each blank with a verb from this list. Use each verb **only once**. Be sure the completed sentences make sense.

VERB LIST

calls	climbs	cuts	drinks	eats
hits	loves	runs	rushes	works

1. Fred _____ baseballs very hard.

2. Larry _____ fast.

3. The fire engine _____ to fires several times a day.

4. Flores _____ all the time.

5. Marie _____ the lawn every Saturday.

6. Seth _____ mountains for sport.

7. My brother _____ his girlfriend very much.

8. Mario _____ too much beer.

9. She _____ her dinner in front of the television.

10. Noriko _____ her little sister nearly every day.

STOP CHECK ANSWERS ON PAGE 120.

RECOGNIZING ACTION WORDS (VERBS)

Read the following:

call	climb	cut	drink
eat	go	hit	love
run	rush	walk	work

Did you notice?

Each of the words is an action word, or verb.

Do you remember?

Action words, or verbs, give part of the meaning to sentences. They let you know what action a sentence tells about.

Try it out.

Here are ten rows of words. Circle each of the action words.

1.	play	child	cry	work
2.	jump	happy	factory	sky
3.	build	joy	same	woman
4.	person	sell	kind	climb
5.	nice	meat	fight	run
6.	kiss	drink	save	silly
7.	me	one	help	see
8.	fruit	money	hair	eat
9.	sit	airplane	idea	lady
10.	seven	hurt	heavy	good

STOP   CHECK ANSWERS ON PAGE 120.

THE WORDS *A* AND *AN*

Did you know?

The letters **a, e, i, o, u,** and sometimes **y** are vowels.
All the other letters of the alphabet are consonants.
When it begins a word, the letter **y** is a consonant.

Read the following:

a book	a cat	a dog	a fan	a girl
a hat	a jail	a kite	a lamp	a man
a name	a park	a queen	a ride	a sail
a tale	a van	a window	a yard	a zoo

Now read the following:

an ape	an apple	an arrow	an egg	an evening
an iron	an inch	an orange	an oven	an uncle

Did you notice?

The word **a** goes before words that begin with consonants.
The word **an** goes before words that begin with vowels.
Both **a** and **an** are used to talk about one person or thing.

Try it out.

Put **a** or **an** before each of the following words.

1. _____ onion

2. _____ fox

3. _____ worker

4. _____ yell

5. _____ dress

6. _____ door

7. _____ coat

8. _____ undertaker

9. _____ fire

10. _____ pea

11. _____ earring

12. _____ ant

13. _____ pan

14. _____ seat

15. _____ apron

16. _____ wolf

17. _____ illness

18. _____ knife

19. _____ name

20. _____ store

STOP CHECK ANSWERS ON PAGE 120.

THE ALPHABET

Read the following:

a b c d e f g h i j k l m n o p q r s t u v w x y z

Now read the following:

apple	big	cat	dear	even	fat	girl
home	ice	jail	kite	land	mouse	name
on	put	queen	red	sat	time	us
very	was	x-ray	young	zoo		

Did you notice?

The words are listed in the order of the alphabet.

Try it out.

Write the following pairs of words in the order of the alphabet. An example shows you how to do it. Write each word in a blank.

1. seat   floor   *floor*   *seat*

2. egg   milk   _____   _____

3. factory   work   _____   _____

4. sad   happy   _____   _____

5. mean   large   _____   _____

6. work   play   _____   _____

7. sour   apple   _____   _____

8. can   bear   _____   _____

9. pet   dog   _____   _____

10. pay   wish   _____   _____

STOP   CHECK ANSWERS ON PAGE 120.

THE ALPHABET

Read the following:

sick   bad   happy

Now read the following:

bad   happy   sick

Did you notice?

The first list is not in the order of the alphabet.
The second list is in alphabetical order: **b**ad, **h**appy, **s**ick

Try it out.

Write the following groups of words in alphabetical order.

1. man, woman, child   _____ _____ _____

2. tall, big, happy   _____ _____ _____

3. milk, butter, tired   _____ _____ _____

4. finger, open, boil   _____ _____ _____

5. one, an, team   _____ _____ _____

6. large, dry, ant   _____ _____ _____

7. part, hat, top   _____ _____ _____

8. red, brown, green   _____ _____ _____

9. send, mean, tell   _____ _____ _____

10. fire, boss, men   _____ _____ _____

STOP   CHECK ANSWERS ON PAGE 120.

CAPITAL LETTERS

Write the following sentences over. Use capital letters correctly.

1. allen moore and i are friends with josé and mike.

   _____

2. tony rizzoli, bob grant, and i are good friends.

   _____

3. sara washington and i work well together.

   _____

4. my friend keung chan does not like my other friend dan davis.

   _____

5. fred, gary, claude, and i bowl together.

   _____

TELLING AND ASKING SENTENCES

Write the following sentences over. Use correct capital letters and end marks.

1. did teresa leave her husband again

   _____

2. how do you like your new boss

   _____

3. the people at my office are not happy

   _____

4. is that fair

   _____

5. my friends sharon, giovanna, florence, and eileen will be there

   _____

GO ON TO THE NEXT PAGE

6. what are you doing with my car

_____

7. i want to visit my friend ruth travis

_____

8. how much do i owe you

_____

9. why should i do that

_____

10. all my buddies are going on a hunting trip

_____

RECOGNIZING NAMING WORDS (NOUNS)

Draw a line under the naming word, or noun, in each sentence.

1. His wife works too hard.
2. Our house is very cold.
3. We bought new furniture.
4. My father lives here now.
5. The country is beautiful.

MORE THAN ONE (PLURAL)

Add an **s** or **es** ending to any noun that needs one.

1. both kitten
2. a drink
3. six pass
4. some kiss
5. two test

6. a bat
7. all bet
8. four glass
9. an apple
10. several girl

GO ON TO THE NEXT PAGE

RECOGNIZING ACTION WORDS (VERBS)

Put a line under the action word, or verb, in each sentence.

1. My dog wags its tail at people.

2. His dog growls at other animals.

3. My dog Alfie never bites.

4. He plays very well with children.

5. Alfie also protects the children from strangers.

THE WORDS *A* AND *AN*

Put **a** or **an** before each of the following words.

1. _____ child   6. _____ hat

2. _____ elevator   7. _____ actress

3. _____ island   8. _____ dam

4. _____ door   9. _____ party

5. _____ chicken   10. _____ boat

THE ALPHABET

Write the following groups of words in alphabetical order.

1. friend, cheerful, tired   _____ _____ _____

2. pretty, nice, also   _____ _____ _____

3. seal, make, bread   _____ _____ _____

4. gone, deep, mean   _____ _____ _____

5. let, tan, do   _____ _____ _____

STOP CHECK ANSWERS BEGINNING ON PAGE 119.

PROGRESS CHART CHAPTER ONE REVIEW

Count how many items you answered correctly in each **Section** of the Chapter One Review. Write your score per section in the **My Scores** column. If all of your section scores are as high as the **Good Scores,** go on to Chapter Two. If any of your section scores are lower than the **Good Scores,** study the lessons on the assigned **Review Pages** again before you go on to Chapter Two.

Section	Good Scores	My Scores	Review Pages
Capital Letters	4 or 5		2–3
Telling and Asking Sentences	8, 9, or 10		4–6
Recognizing Naming Words (Nouns)	4 or 5		8–9
More Than One (Plural)	8, 9, or 10		10–11
Recognizing Action Words (Verbs)	4 or 5		12–13
The Words **A** and **An**	8, 9, or 10		14
The Alphabet	4 or 5		15–16

CAPITAL LETTERS

Read the following:

Sharon and David are getting married.
Both David and I have brothers and sisters.

Do you remember?

People's names begin with capital letters.
Sentences begin with capital letters.
The word **I** is written with a capital letter.

Try it out.

Write these sentences over. Use capital letters correctly.

1. mary and i refuse to go if jerry goes.

_____

2. will flores and steve be there?

_____

3. who will bring mino and sarah to the wedding?

_____

4. did i tell you about eleni's new job?

_____

5. i only know that mehdi, julie, and i are going.

_____

STOP CHECK ANSWERS ON PAGE 121.

CAPITAL LETTERS FOR DAYS OF THE WEEK

Read the following:

Here are the names of the seven days of the week:

Sunday	Wednesday	Friday
Monday	Thursday	Saturday
Tuesday		

Did you notice?

The names of the days in the week begin with capital letters.

Try it out.

Fill in the blanks with the days of the week.

1. The first day of the week is Sunday; the third day is _____.

2. The last day of the week is _____.

3. Friday comes after _____.

4. The sixth day of the week is _____.

5. Saturday comes before _____.

6. The seventh day of the week is _____.

7. Sunday comes before _____.

8. Thursday comes after _____.

9. The five weekdays are _____, _____,

   _____, _____, and _____.

10. The two days of the weekend are _____ and _____.

STOP CHECK ANSWERS ON PAGE 121.

TELLING AND ASKING SENTENCES

Read the following:

My friend and I love to travel.
Why did you make reservations for that day?

Did you notice?

The first sentence is a telling sentence, or a statement.
The second sentence is an asking sentence, or a question.

Do you remember?

All sentences begin with capital letters.
Statements end with periods (.).
Some questions begin with **who, what, when, where, why,** or **how**.
Some other questions begin with **is, are, do,** or **have**.
Questions end with question marks (**?**).

Try it out.

Write the following sentences over. Use correct capital letters and end marks.

1. i have not been on a plane before

   _____

2. how much will the ticket cost me

   _____

3. not one person will go in my place

   _____

4. are you going to wear that on the trip

   _____

5. who will meet us at the airport

   _____

STOP CHECK ANSWERS ON PAGE 121.

TELLING AND ASKING SENTENCES

Read the following:

My best friend is getting married.
When is the wedding?

Did you notice?

The first sentence is a statement.
The second sentence is a question.

Do you remember?

Statements tell something.
They end with periods (.).
Questions ask something.
They end with question marks (?).

Try it out.

Write the following sentences over. Use correct capital letters and end marks.

1. the wedding is next sunday

   _____

2. will marie and derek be invited

   _____

3. janice said that i will be in the wedding party

   _____

4. what are you and judy wearing

   _____

5. how old is the groom

   _____

6. i heard that the bride is two years older than the groom

   _____

GO ON TO THE NEXT PAGE.

7. the groom is a nice person

_____

8. is this the first time he has been married

_____

9. it is the second marriage for both

_____

10. do they have any children

_____

STOP CHECK ANSWERS ON PAGE 121.

END MARKS

Do you remember?

Every sentence must have an end mark.
A telling sentence, or statement, ends with a period (.).
An asking sentence, or question, ends with a question mark (**?**).

Try it out.

Put the correct end mark at the end of each sentence.

1. Are you bringing her here

2. My family does not like her

3. Why is she so mean

4. Do not believe a word she says

5. She lies about everything

6. How can she lie like that

7. Do you think she ever tells the truth

8. Nobody knows the truth about her

9. Let me tell you what she has done

10. It is not fair to talk about her now

STOP CHECK ANSWERS ON PAGE 121.

WORD ORDER IN SENTENCES

Read the following:

Don and Sing work with me.
Them I work with like to.
I like to work with them.

Did you notice?

The second group of words does not make sense.
The words are not in correct order.
The first and third groups of words make sense.
The words in each are in correct order. They make sentences.

Did you know?

For a sentence to make sense, the words must be in correct order.

Try it out.

Write the following groups of words over. Write sentences that make sense.
Put the words in correct order.

1. Ten working I been for have years.

   _____

2. Jobs would change I like to.

   _____

3. Know to how I don't this do.

   _____

4. Wife work my does not to go.

   _____

5. Home wants stay to she children with the.

   _____

STOP   CHECK ANSWERS ON PAGE 121.

WORD ORDER IN SENTENCES

Read the following:

He she are and warm.

Did you notice?

The above group of words does not make sense.
The words are not in correct order.
In correct order the words would make a sentence:

He and she are warm.

Do you remember?

The word order must be correct for a sentence to make sense.

Try it out.

Write the following groups of words over. Write sentences that make sense.
Put the words in correct order.

1. To I car work a drive.

   _____

2. Do where you live?

   _____

3. Are going you where?

   _____

4. Swimming sport my best is.

   _____

5. Best Marie friend my is.

   _____

STOP CHECK ANSWERS ON PAGE 121.

NAMING WORDS (NOUNS)

Read the following:

brother	cow	book	barn
girl	horse	night	bedroom
man	pig	oven	lake

Did you notice?

All the words are naming words, or nouns.
The words name persons, animals, things, and places.

Now read the following:

The naming words, or nouns, are underlined in these sentences.
    The white <u>cat</u> is drinking its <u>milk</u>.
    The shaggy <u>dog</u> barks at <u>people</u>.

Try it out.

Fill in each blank with a noun from this list. Use each noun **only once.** Be sure the completed sentences make sense.

NOUN LIST

boy	bus	child	friend	girl
house	lunch	money	school	wife

1. I have a seven-year-old _____.

2. My daughter is a pretty _____.

3. My friend's son is a nice _____.

4. They are both in _____.

5. They ride the _____ every morning.

6. They eat _____ in school at noon.

7. My _____, Mary, and I work in offices.

8. Mary's _____ Sally watches our children after school.

9. Mary and I need the _____ we both earn to pay the bills.

10. We want to buy a _____ someday.

STOP CHECK ANSWERS ON PAGE 121.

RECOGNIZING NAMING WORDS (NOUNS)

Do you remember?

Words such as **mother, man, dog, lion, book, ball, house, mercy, honor, happiness,** and **fear** are naming words, or nouns.
All the words name persons, animals, things, places, ideas, or feelings.

Read the following:

The large truck hit a bump in the road.

Did you notice?

There are three nouns in that sentence.
This is the same sentence with the nouns underlined:

The large truck hit a bump in the road.

Try it out.

Draw a line under each noun in the following sentences. Some sentences have two nouns.

1. My father is not working.

2. His union voted for a strike.

3. The workers can't afford to be out of work.

4. My mother is very worried.

5. The family does not have very much money.

6. I have three brothers and two sisters.

7. My mother works at home.

8. This strike is hurting my family.

9. Are the workers striking for more money?

10. Do the owners want the strike?

STOP CHECK ANSWERS ON PAGE 122.

MORE THAN ONE (PLURAL)

Do you remember?

Some nouns name more than one person, animal, thing, place, idea, or feeling.

Those nouns are **plural nouns**.

Many plural nouns end with **s**: dog**s**, cat**s**, girl**s**, brother**s**, and apple**s**.

Some singular nouns end with **s** or **ss**: bus, hiss, mess, stress.

Those nouns end with **es** when they are plural: bus**es**, hiss**es**, mess**es**, stress**es**.

Try it out.

Add an **s** or **es** ending to any noun that needs one.

1. five pear
2. a book
3. both glass
4. some nail

5. two test
6. ten banana
7. several dress

8. two class
9. five kiss
10. three bus

STOP   CHECK ANSWERS ON PAGE 122.

MORE THAN ONE (PLURAL)

Read the following:

a bench	five bench**es**
one brush	two brush**es**
a bush	three bush**es**
one church	six church**es**

Did you notice?

Some singular nouns end with **sh** or **ch**.
Those nouns end with **es** when they are plural.

Do you remember?

Singular nouns name one person, animal, thing, place, idea, or feeling.
Plural nouns name more than one.

Try it out.

Add an **s** or **es** ending to any noun that needs one.

1. some glove
2. three fence
3. many dish
4. two lash

5. both ranch
6. three wish
7. a lock

8. several crash
9. four plant
10. five wash

STOP CHECK ANSWERS ON PAGE 122.

ACTION WORDS (VERBS)

Read the following:
play talk walk work

Did you notice?
Each of the words is an action word, or verb.

Do you remember?
Action words, or verbs, give part of the meaning to sentences.

Try it out.

Fill in each blank with a verb from this list. Use each verb **only once**. Be sure the completed sentences make sense.

VERB LIST

believes	cares	drives	goes	grows
helps	hits	plays	sings	spells

1. My brother always _____ with the radio.

2. That player _____ the ball too hard.

3. Veldez _____ the piano very well.

4. No one _____ her story.

5. Lisa _____ tomatoes in her garden.

6. At work Jerry _____ his friend a lot.

7. Brigitte _____ a lot about people.

8. Kim _____ a nice car.

9. This child _____ his name correctly.

10. Steve _____ to the school his father attended.

STOP CHECK ANSWERS ON PAGE 122.

RECOGNIZING ACTION WORDS (VERBS)

Read the following:

Wagdy <u>loves</u> movies.
He always <u>tells</u> his friends about each scene.
He <u>describes</u> the scenes excitedly.

Did you notice?

In each sentence a word is underlined.
Those words are actions words, or verbs.

Do you remember?

Verbs give part of the meaning to sentences.
Verbs let you know what actions the sentences tell about.

Try it out.

Draw a line under the action word, or verb, in each sentence.

1. In the movie, the woman screams at the robber.

2. The robber pushes people out of the way.

3. One woman falls.

4. Another person hurts his head.

5. Someone helps the police.

6. One man catches the robber.

7. He hits him with a stick.

8. A police officer handcuffs the robber.

9. The robber curses at the police.

10. Another police officer returns the pocketbook to the woman.

STOP CHECK ANSWERS ON PAGE 122.

THE ALPHABET

Read the following:
ill   health   sad   well

Now read the following:
health   ill   sad   well

Did you notice?
Only the second list is in the order of the alphabet.

Try it out.
Write the following groups of words in alphabetical order.

1. pretty, cost, happy, good

   _____   _____   _____   _____

2. in, out, off, at

   _____   _____   _____   _____

3. nine, eight, seven, five

   _____   _____   _____   _____

4. fight, peace, sell, hope

   _____   _____   _____   _____

5. red, green, yellow, purple

   _____   _____   _____   _____

STOP   CHECK ANSWERS ON PAGE 122.

CAPITAL LETTERS

Write these sentences over. Use capital letters correctly.

1. mohammed and i are meeting on tuesday.

   _____

2. my boss makes us work on saturdays.

   _____

3. i only work on mondays, wednesdays, and fridays.

   _____

4. my brothers mike, patrick, and i do not work on sundays.

   _____

5. james washington and i have a date next thursday.

   _____

TELLING AND ASKING SENTENCES

Write the following sentences over. Use correct capital letters and end marks.

1. who drove my car yesterday

   _____

2. i cannot understand that

   _____

3. why would you do such a thing

   _____

4. where are you staying now

   _____

5. is that the correct way to do it

   _____

GO ON TO THE NEXT PAGE

6. jim and i are getting married

_____

7. we are having a small wedding

_____

8. will you come to it

_____

9. our parents want a big affair

_____

10. how much will this cost us

_____

WORD ORDER IN SENTENCES

Write the following groups of words over. Write sentences that make sense.
Put the words in correct order.

1. Couples we inviting party are two our to.

_____

2. Married and I have Peter year been one for.

_____

3. Dated friends five for our years.

_____

4. Divorce a José Sally just and got.

_____

5. Unhappy are very children their.

_____

RECOGNIZING NAMING WORDS (NOUNS)

Draw a line under each noun in the following sentences.

1. The frightened animals in the cave moved slowly.

2. A large snake climbed the tree in its cage at the zoo.

3. One person put her hand inside the cage.

GO ON TO THE NEXT PAGE

4. The zookeeper yelled at the woman.

5. My friend wanted to see the lions and the apes.

MORE THAN ONE (PLURAL)

Add an **s** or **es** ending to any noun that needs one.

1. ten cake
2. both letter
3. two wish
4. nine brush

5. several church
6. four pass
7. a beach

8. three witch
9. some match
10. a bag

RECOGNIZING ACTION WORDS (VERBS)

Draw a line under the action word, or verb, in each sentence.

1. In the movie, the hunter moves quietly and quickly.

2. He turns his head at every sound.

3. The hunter jumps from a tree.

4. The deer runs away.

5. The hunter yells at the deer.

THE ALPHABET

Write the following groups of words in alphabetical order.

1. sat, man, hat, coat

_____ _____ _____ _____

2. girl, woman, child, lamb

_____ _____ _____ _____

3. young, quick, fire, tie

_____ _____ _____ _____

4. tiny, king, eat, us

_____ _____ _____ _____

5. see, my, was, pet

_____ _____ _____ _____

STOP CHECK ANSWERS BEGINNING ON PAGE 122.

Count how many items you answered correctly in each **Section** of the Chapter Two Review. Write your score per section in the **My Scores** column. If all of your section scores are as high as the **Good Scores,** go on to Chapter Three. If any of your section scores are lower than the **Good Scores,** study the lessons on the assigned **Review Pages** again before you go on to Chapter Three.

Section	Good Scores	My Scores	Review Pages
Capital Letters	4 or 5		22–23
Telling and Asking Sentences	8, 9, or 10		24–26
Word Order in Sentences	4 or 5		28–29
Recognizing Naming Words (Nouns)	4 or 5		30–31
More Than One (Plural)	8, 9, or 10		32–33
Recognizing Action Words (Verbs)	4 or 5		34–35
The Alphabet	4 or 5		36

CHAPTER THREE

CAPITAL LETTERS FOR MONTHS OF THE YEAR

Read the following:

Here are the names of the months of the year.

January	February	March	April
May	June	July	August
September	October	November	December

Did you notice?

The name of each month begins with a capital letter.

Try it out.

Write the name of a month in each blank.

1. What is the fifth month of the year? _____

2. What month comes after January? _____

3. What is the eleventh month of the year? _____

4. What month comes before October? _____

5. What is the first month of the year? _____

6. What month comes before April? _____

7. What month comes after July? _____

8. What month comes after November? _____

9. What is the fourth month of the year? _____

10. What is the tenth month of the year? _____

STOP CHECK ANSWERS ON PAGE 123.

TELLING AND ASKING SENTENCES

Read the following:

_____ said that?

_____ refuses to go tonight.

Now read the following:

One of these words belongs in each blank in the sentences above:
   He   Who
The first sentence is a question.
Who goes in the blank.
The completed sentence says: **Who said that?**
The second sentence is a statement.
The completed sentence says: **He refuses to go tonight.**

Try it out.

Fill in each blank with a word from this list. Use each word **only once**. Be sure the completed sentences make sense.

WORD LIST

how	husband	jail	police	shelter
what	when	where	who	why

1. _____ is she so frightened?

2. _____ happened yesterday?

3. Her _____ beat her yesterday.

4. _____ told you all this?

5. My friend called the _____ .

6. _____ did they take him.

7. They took him to _____ .

8. She slept in a _____ .

9. _____ is she coming home?

10. _____ long have they been married?

STOP CHECK ANSWERS ON PAGE 123.

WORD ORDER IN SENTENCES

Read the following:

Hank going where is?

Did you notice?

The sentence does not make sense.
It should say this:

Where is Hank going?

Do you remember?

For a sentence to make sense, the words must be in correct order.
A sentence begins with a capital letter.
An asking sentence ends with a question mark (**?**).

Try it out.

Write the following groups of words over. Write questions that make sense.
Put the words in correct order.

1. Always Hank are boss fighting his why and?

   _____

2. Worked has Hank long how here?

   _____

3. Fired or Hank did get did quit he?

   _____

4. Job Hank able get will be to another?

   _____

5. Family how he live will and his?

   _____

STOP CHECK ANSWERS ON PAGE 123.

NAMING WORDS (NOUNS)

Read the following:

These words are all of the same type:
   student, worker, mouse, bear, bread, desk, beach, school, courage, beauty, sadness, joy

Did you notice?

All of the words are nouns. Each of them names a person, an animal, a thing, a place, an idea, or a feeling.

Try it out.

Some of the nouns are missing from the following short story. Fill in each blank in the story with a noun from this list. Use each noun **only once**. Be sure the completed story makes sense.

NOUN LIST

army	friends	home	houses	jobs
money	school	uncle	world	years

Bob and Bill had been _____ for ten _____. They
(1)   (2)

went to the same _____. They always had the same
(3)

_____ after school. Now, everything was changed. Bob was going
(4)

into the _____. Bill was not. Bill was going to work for his
(5)

_____. He was going to build _____. He would earn a
(6)   (7)

lot of _____. Bob wanted Bill to come with him to see the
(8)

_____. Bill wanted Bob to stay _____.
(9)   (10)

STOP CHECK ANSWERS ON PAGE 123.

RECOGNIZING NAMING WORDS (NOUNS)

Read the following:

| bee | burglar | carrot | cat | crying |
| happiness | new | running | seat | toy |

Did you notice?

The naming words, or nouns, in the list above are underlined.

Do you remember?

Nouns name persons, animals, things, places, ideas, or feelings.

Try it out.

Here are ten rows of words. Circle each of the naming words, or nouns.

1. castle   careful   name   red

2. big   grown   child   water

3. hear   damp   see   face

4. fire   fixing   sure   happy

5. house   woman   near   jumping

6. saved   bank   log   number

7. never   held   cried   maid

8. building   room   dry   cold

9. grow   tub   butter   anger

10. have   is   grew   chicken

STOP   CHECK ANSWERS ON PAGE 123.

MORE THAN ONE (PLURAL)

Did you know?

People's names can be plural.
Two people named Rosa are two Rosas.

Read the following:

one Flores	two Floreses
one Nomura	two Nomuras
one Burns	two Burnses
one Smith	two Smiths

Did you notice?

The endings on plural names are like the endings on other plural nouns.

Many plural names end with **s**: George**s**, Kim**s**, Olivia**s**.

Some singular names end with **s**, **ss**, **ch**, or **sh**: Davi**s**, Be**ss**, Ri**ch**, Ti**sh**.

Those names end with **es** when they are plural: Davis**es**, Bess**es**, Rich**es**, Tish**es**.

Do you remember?

Naming words such as goat, hat, book, desk, and dance end with **s** when they are plural.

Singular nouns that end with **s** and **ss** end with **es** when they are plural.

Singular nouns that end with **ch** and **sh** also end with **es** when they are plural.

Try it out.

Add an **s** or **es** ending to any naming word, or noun, that needs one.

1. many cat	6. six fence	11. two Brown	16. seven George
2. two bush	7. several match	12. five Charles	17. two princess
3. a few card	8. the carpet	13. two Jones	18. five button
4. a bed	9. all boss	14. both Barbero	19. some branch
5. ten wish	10. three glass	15. two Green	20. four Wong

STOP CHECK ANSWERS ON PAGE 123.

THE WORDS *HE*, *SHE*, AND *IT* (PRONOUNS)

Read the following:

Gary works too hard.
He needs a rest.

In the second sentence, **he** is used in place of **Gary**.

Now read the following:

My sister loves her work.
She is a social worker.

In the second sentence, **she** is used in place of **sister**.

Now read the following:

The chair is too hard.
It needs a pillow.

In the second sentence, **it** is used in place of **chair**.

Did you notice?

The words **he**, **she**, and **it** are used in place of nouns.

Now read the following:

We need to choose a **captain** for our bowling team.
He or she should be a good player.

When it is not clear if the person referred to is a man or a woman, the words **he or she** are used.

Did you know?

Words that take the place of naming words, or nouns, are called **pronouns**.

Try it out.

Fill in each blank sentence with **he**, **she**, **it**, or **he or she**.

1. My brother Jim is coming back home.

    _____ will try to help us.

GO ON TO THE NEXT PAGE

2. Our club must elect a new treasurer.

_____ must attend every meeting.

3. My mother is a good cook.

_____ makes everything my father likes.

4. The car we own is very old.

_____ needs lots of repairs.

5. My mother is looking for a job.

_____ doesn't want my father to worry.

STOP CHECK ANSWERS ON PAGE 123.

DESCRIBING WORDS (ADJECTIVES)

Read the following:

The cat is running.
The small, shaggy white cat is running.

Did you notice?

The second sentence has words that describe the cat.
It gives more information about the cat.
The words **small**, **shaggy**, and **white** describe the cat.

Now read the following:

Describing words make sentences more interesting.
Here are some words that are used to describe naming words.

bad	fat	funny	good	happy
large	mean	nice	poor	rich

You probably know many more such words.

Did you know?

Words that describe naming words, or nouns, are called **adjectives**.

Try it out.

Here are five sentences with blanks. Write one adjective in each blank.
Choose the best word to describe the naming words in the sentences.

1. My _____ sweater has _____ holes in it.

   (tall, high, old, silly, big)

2. The _____ man walked with a _____ cane.

   (ripe, crooked, dry, tired, sunny)

3. A _____ woman dressed in _____ clothes called for

   help. **(plenty, large, spicy, torn, fake)**

4. The _____ lady and the _____ man laughed at the

   _____ sight. **(green, pretty, high, low, funny, handsome)**

5. No one saw the _____ dog enter the _____ store.

   (blue, rich, new, black, fresh)

STOP   CHECK ANSWERS ON PAGE 123.

RECOGNIZING DESCRIBING WORDS (ADJECTIVES)

Read the following:

Here are some adjectives, or describing words:

dry, fat, green, nice, old, pretty, short, tall, thin, young

Now read the following:

Here are some adjectives in sentences:

Ann is a **pretty** woman.

Gary is a **good** father.

Do you remember?

A noun names a person, animal, thing, place, idea, or feeling. Other words describe persons, animals, things, places, ideas, or feelings.

Those words are called **adjectives**.

Try it out.

Here are ten sentences. Draw lines under all the words that describe naming words.

1. Anne is an excellent cook.

2. Gary always has hot meals for dinner.

3. A mean woman yelled at their child.

4. Did Gary buy that large white cat?

5. His large, fluffy fat cat eats too much.

6. Anne drinks hot tea in the morning.

7. She does not like dirty floors.

8. Anne is a caring person.

9. Gary is a kind man.

10. He takes his son to nice places.

STOP CHECK ANSWERS ON PAGE 123.

THE WORDS *AM, ARE,* AND *IS*

Read the following:

I **am** here.	We **are** here.
You **are** here.	You **are** here.
He **is** here.	They **are** here.
She **is** here.	They **are** here.
It **is** here.	They **are** here.

Now read the following:

The words **am**, **are**, and **is** are used often.
It is important to use them correctly.

Try it out.

Fill in each blank with **am**, **are**, or **is**.

1. It _____ hot today.

2. I _____ happy.

3. She _____ not a nice person.

4. How _____ you?

5. _____ they here yet?

6. _____ it time to leave?

7. You _____ too young to go.

8. _____ he your teacher?

9. She _____ my mother.

10. You _____ lucky.

STOP CHECK ANSWERS ON PAGE 123.

THE WORDS AM, ARE, AND IS

Read the following:

José **is** nice.   Sam and Bob **are** brothers.
Yoshiko **is** young.   Sue and Cindy **are** sisters.
The child **is** pretty.   The flowers **are** in bloom.

Did you notice?

The word **is** is used when one person or one thing is named.
The word **are** is used when more than one person or thing is named.

Do you remember?

The word **am** is used with the word **I**.
The word **is** is used with the words **he**, **she**, and **it**.
The word **are** is used with the words **you**, **we**, and **they**.

Try it out.

Here are ten sentences with blanks. Fill in each blank with **am**, **are**, or **is**.

1. Jason _____ always late.

2. Marty and Pat _____ at home.

3. The birds _____ in my yard.

4. I _____ not sure about that.

5. Veronica _____ my best friend.

6. Carole and I _____ not going.

7. Why _____ you not going?

8. _____ Herb and Ling coming home tonight?

9. Snow _____ falling right now.

10. It _____ too cold for me.

STOP CHECK ANSWERS ON PAGE 123.

ACTION WORDS (VERBS)

Read the following:

Tony <u>works</u>.   Tony and Joanna <u>work</u>.
Alice <u>sings</u> well.   Alice and Jeff <u>sing</u> well.
The apple <u>tastes</u> good.   The apples <u>taste</u> good.
The cat <u>meows</u>.   The cats <u>meow</u>.

Did you notice?

Action words end with **s** when they tell about one person or thing.

Try it out.

Write the correct action words, or verbs, in the blanks.

1. Laurent (**bakes** or **bake**) cakes.   _____

2. Noriko and Mino (**drives** or **drive**)
   to work.   _____

3. Pina (**smiles** or **smile**) nicely.   _____

4. Hossein and I (**dances** or **dance**) well.   _____

5. Seth (**works** or **work**) hard.   _____

6. Sharon and Ashok (**likes** or **like**) to
   swim.   _____

7. Carol and Jennifer (**plays** or **play**)
   the piano.   _____

8. The old man (**walks** or **walk**) slowly.   _____

9. The people (**stares** or **stare**) at us.   _____

10. The fresh air (**helps** or **help**) me.   _____

STOP CHECK ANSWERS ON PAGE 123.

ACTION WORDS AND HELPING WORDS (VERBS)

Do you remember?

Words such as **go**, **play**, **grow**, **talk**, **ride**, **rain**, and **sing** are action words.

Read the following:

I am going to school tomorrow.   We are going to school tomorrow.
You are not singing.   You are not singing.
He is talking too much.   They are talking too much.
The plant is growing nicely.   The plants are growing nicely.

Did you notice?

The words **am**, **are**, and **is** can be used with action words.

Did you know?

The words **am**, **are**, and **is** are called **helping words**, or **helping verbs**, when they are used with action words.

Try it out.

Here are ten sentences with blanks. Fill in each blank with **am**, **are**, or **is**.

1. I _____ not working today.

2. Jerry and Françoise _____ staying late tonight.

3. His work _____ his life.

4. Those people _____ waiting for seats.

5. _____ I next?

6. How old _____ you?

7. I _____ not happy because Nick _____ driving.

8. He _____ a poor driver.

9. The factory _____ closed.

10. Giorgio and Karen _____ holding hands.

STOP CHECK ANSWERS ON PAGE 124.

THE ALPHABET

Read the following:

dear, camp, fire, sharp, burn, after, pain, ear

Now read the following:

after, burn, camp, dear, ear, fire, pain, sharp

Did you notice?

Only the second list is in the order of the alphabet.

Try it out.

Write the following groups of words in alphabetical order.
Put commas between the words in the lists you write.

1. pink, green, red, white, brown, yellow, orange, tan

   _____

   _____

2. one, five, seven, eight, two, nine, hundred, million

   _____

   _____

3. tired, ice, mean, sad, happy, good, bad, useful

   _____

   _____

4. grape, lemon, apple, raisin, fruit, pear, orange, banana

   _____

   _____

5. king, queen, prince, worker, helper, boss, factory, mine

   _____

   _____

STOP CHECK ANSWERS ON PAGE 124.

CAPITAL LETTERS

Write these sentences over. Use capital letters correctly.

1. mary brown and i are going away in february.

   _____

2. on wednesday jeff, antonio, and i are going on a trip.

   _____

3. october, november and december are my best months.

   _____

4. i like may, june, and july the best.

   _____

5. george, ken, and i are going skiing in january.

   _____

TELLING AND ASKING SENTENCES

Fill in each blank with a word from this list. Use each word **only once**. Be sure the completed sentences make sense.

WORD LIST

are	boss	explorers	how	man
what	when	where	who	why

1. _____ did she leave him?

2. _____ will she do now?

3. _____ told you that story?

4. My _____ is a nice person.

5. The _____ looked at the strange sight.

6. _____ are you going?

7. _____ they coming to the party?

GO ON TO THE NEXT PAGE

8. _____ much do I owe you?

9. That _____ is looking at us.

10. _____ should we get there?

WORD ORDER IN SENTENCES

Write the following groups of words over. Write questions that make sense. Put the words in correct order.

1. New is excited job about Jim his?

_____

2. He where work does?

_____

3. Far you job from live do your?

_____

4. Job like do your you?

_____

5. Looking who new a for is job?

_____

RECOGNIZING NAMING WORD (NOUNS)

Circle each of the naming words, or nouns.

1. book   very   rock   colorful

2. small   child   school   tired

3. red   oven   ear   fresh

4. wife   nice   sit   seat

5. cool   cookie   window   brown

MORE THAN ONE (PLURAL)

Add an **s** or **es** ending to any naming word, or noun, that needs one.

1. some dress	4. four Flores	7. two Johnston	9. two James
2. both ranch	5. many crash	8. two Charles	10. some boat
3. six Jones	6. one Duval		

GO ON TO THE NEXT PAGE

THE WORDS HE, SHE, AND IT (PRONOUNS)

Fill in each blank with **he, she, it,** or **he or she**.

1. José is arriving tomorrow.

   _____ has been gone a long time.

2. Maria wants us to pick José up.

   _____ cannot meet him.

3. The elected candidate will have a hard job.

   _____ will have to work long hours.

4. That man looks funny.

   _____ just ran out of the store.

5. My house needs a good cleaning.

   _____ hasn't been cleaned since Monday.

RECOGNIZING DESCRIBING WORDS (ADJECTIVES)

Draw lines under all the words that describe naming words.

1. The soft, cuddly white kitten meowed.

2. In the long story the mean old woman frightened the child.

3. She is a wonderful person.

4. The robber is a smart person.

5. I love my new green scarf.

THE WORDS AM, ARE, AND IS

Fill in each blank with **am, are,** or **is**.

1. She _____ a happy person.

2. It _____ a nice day.

3. They _____ my best friends.

4. _____ you coming with us?

5. _____ it time to go?

GO ON TO THE NEXT PAGE

6. Felipe and George _____ here.

7. Donna and I _____ not able to go.

8. _____ James going?

9. I _____ a hard worker.

10. Luiz _____ a good boss.

ACTION WORDS (VERBS)

Write the correct action word in the blank.

1. John (**mows** or **mow**) the lawn.   _____

2. Franco and Daniela (**love** or **loves**) their new house.   _____

3. My dog (**lick** or **licks**) my face.   _____

4. Those rocks (**breaks or break**) easily.   _____

5. Dave (**work** or **works**) hard.   _____

6. My windows (**needs** or **need**) washing.   _____

7. Bijan (**drive** or **drives**) too fast.   _____

8. José (**eat** or **eats**) too slowly.   _____

9. Those women (**laughs** or **laugh**) a lot.   _____

10. The peaches (**tastes** or **taste**) good.   _____

ACTION WORDS AND HELPING WORDS (VERBS)

Fill in each blank with **am**, **are**, or **is**.

1. She _____ going on a trip.

2. It _____ raining now.

3. _____ I helping you?

4. Alice _____ doing well.

5. _____ you working today?

GO ON TO THE NEXT PAGE

THE ALPHABET

Write the following groups of words in alphabetical order. Put commas between the words in the lists you write.

1. down, great, zoo, sure, make, use, book, car

_____

_____

2. for, in, pat, an, the, six, open, bar

_____

_____

3. even, you, sell, put, win, bet, are, zebra

_____

_____

4. Beatrice, Seth, Carla, Juan, Ann, Tom, George, Darioush

_____

_____

5. José, Sachiko, Donna, Marie, Tony, Robert, Laura, Arturo

_____

_____

STOP CHECK ANSWERS BEGINNING ON PAGE 124.

Count how many items you answered correctly in each **Section** of the Chapter Three Review. Write your score per section in the **My Scores** column. If all of your section scores are as high as the **Good Scores,** go on to Chapter Four. If any of your section scores are lower than the **Good Scores,** study the lessons on the assigned **Review Pages** again before you go on to Chapter Four.

Section	Good Scores	My Scores	Review Pages
Capital Letters	4 or 5		42
Telling and Asking Sentences	8, 9, or 10		43
Word Order in Sentences	4 or 5		44
Recognizing Naming Words (Nouns)	4 or 5		45–46
More Than One (Plural)	8, 9, or 10		47
The Words **He, She,** and **It** (Pronouns)	4 or 5		48–49
Recognizing Describing Words (Adjectives)	4 or 5		50–51
The Words **Am, Are,** and **Is**	8, 9, or 10		52–53
Action Words (Verbs)	8, 9, or 10		54
Action Words and Helping Words (Verbs)	4 or 5		55
The Alphabet	4 or 5		56

CHAPTER FOUR

CAPITAL LETTERS

Read the following:

Mr. and Mrs. O'Malley like to travel.

Ms. Compton likes to travel too.

Miss Berger is starting to plan for our trip to the country.

Did you notice?

People's titles, such as **Mr.**, **Mrs.**, **Miss**, and **Ms.**, begin with capital letters.

There is a period (.) after **Mr.**, **Mrs.**, and **Ms.**

The title **Miss** does not have a period after it.

Do you remember?

Names such as Alice, Ana, Brigitte, Marie, Medhi, Olivier, and Ricardo begin with capital letters.

Every sentence begins with a capital letter.

The word **I** is written with a capital letter.

Try it out.

Write the following sentences over. Use capital letters correctly.

1. mr. and mrs. parsons and their daughter susan live there.

   _____

2. bob, hideo, kim, and i know mr. grant will want to come.

   _____

3. my cousins pat and sharon are visiting mrs. salazar that weekend.

   _____

4. miss carone and i are going to drive.

   _____

5. ms. lombardi, her sister sharee, and i own a van.

   _____

STOP CHECK ANSWERS ON PAGE 125.

TELLING AND ASKING SENTENCES

Read the following:

My _____ asked me to work late last night
_____ will I tell my girlfriend

Now read the following:

One of these words belongs in each blank in the sentences above:
  what   boss
Both sentences need end marks.
The first sentence tells something.
The word **boss** goes in the blank.
The sentence ends with a period (.).
The completed sentence says: **My boss asked me to work late last night.**
The second sentence is a question.
What goes in the blank.
The end mark is a question mark (?).
The completed sentence says: **What will I tell my girlfriend?**

Do you remember?

Asking sentences often begin with words such as the following:
  who, what, when, where, why, or **how**

Try it out.

Fill in each blank with a word from this list. Use each word **only once**. Add an end mark to each sentence. Be sure the completed sentences make sense.

WORD LIST

dog	friend	how	swimmer	truck
what	when	where	why	works

1. _____ old are you

2. _____ are you going tonight

3. My _____ is angry with me

4. His _____ barks at everyone

GO ON TO THE NEXT PAGE

5. _____ will your train arrive at the station

6. The _____ hit the walker

7. _____ do I have to do that

8. _____ did you do last night

9. Theodore _____ hard

10. Camille is a _____

STOP CHECK ANSWERS ON PAGE 125.

WORD ORDER IN SENTENCES

Read the following:

Little its drinks the milk cat white.

Did you notice?

The sentence does not make sense.
It should say this:

The little white cat drinks its milk.

Do you remember?

For a sentence to make sense, the words must be in correct order.

Try it out.

Use the following groups of words to write sentences. Put the words in correct order.

1. Day the is first work of hard.

   _____

2. Have at three work people name last my.

   _____

3. At visited yesterday James the us office.

   _____

4. Sandwiches ate three I lunch at.

   _____

5. Boss two today people my fired.

   _____

STOP CHECK ANSWERS ON PAGE 125.

SENTENCE PARTS

Did you know?

Sentences have two parts.

The **naming part** tells who or what does the action.

The **action part** tells what the naming part does.

Read the following:

NAMING PART   ACTION PART

The driver   makes deliveries every day.

In the sentence, **The driver** does the action.

The action part of the sentence tells what the driver does: he or she **makes deliveries every day.**

Do you remember?

When a noun names one person or one thing, the verb ends with **s.**

Try it out.

Find the words from Group Two, the action part, that go with each naming part from Group One. Write the letter in the blank.

GROUP ONE (NAMING PART)   **GROUP TWO** (ACTION PART)

____ **1.** Snow   **a.** work at the same place.

____ **2.** Tony and Maria   **b.** plays the piano well.

____ **3.** The cats   **c.** turn toward the sun.

____ **4.** The mailperson   **d.** climbs trees.

____ **5.** Wanda   **e.** play with toys.

____ **6.** Some plants   **f.** tastes good.

____ **7.** Children   **g.** barks at trains.

____ **8.** An ape   **h.** falls silently.

____ **9.** This apple   **i.** meow too much.

____ **10.** My dog   **j.** delivers mail.

STOP   CHECK ANSWERS ON PAGE 125.

WRITING SENTENCES

Read the following:

Tim _____ a _____ store.
His wife _____ son _____ there.

Now read the following:

One of these words belongs in each blank in the sentences above.
  and   work   has   new

Did you notice?

The sentences should be completed this way:
  Tim has a new store.
  His wife and son work there.

Try it out.

Fill in each blank with a word from this list. Use each word **only once**. Be sure the completed sentences make sense.

WORD LIST

are	early	late	many	morning
night	son	store	things	tired

1. Tim, his wife, and his son sell many _____ in their new

   _____ .

2. Tim, his wife, and his _____ work _____ hours.

3. They open the store _____ in the _____ .

4. They close the store _____ at _____ .

5. They _____ very _____ when they get home.

STOP CHECK ANSWERS ON PAGE 125.

NAMING WORDS (NOUNS)

Do you remember?

Naming words, or nouns, name persons, animals, things, places, ideas, or feelings.
Naming words are words such as the following:
   lady, lion, gift, city, happiness, baby, frog, color, office, idea

Try it out.

Fill in each blank with a noun from this list. Use each word **only once**. Be sure the completed sentences make sense.

NOUN LIST

boss	car	family	letter	money
presents	state	time	trip	weeks

1. Carlos and his wife are saving _____.

2. They want to visit their _____.

3. Carlos and his wife want to buy a _____.

4. They want to travel to another _____.

5. They want to leave in a few _____.

6. Carlos spoke to his _____ at work.

7. Carlos and his wife are excited about their _____.

8. They are buying _____ for everybody.

9. They have waited a long _____ for this.

10. They sent a _____ to tell everyone when they would arrive.

STOP CHECK ANSWERS ON PAGE 125.

MORE THAN ONE (PLURAL)

Read the following:

Both pan are boiling.
That cars needs to be fixed.

Did you notice?

The nouns in those sentences are not correct.
The correct sentences are these:

Both pans are boiling.
That car needs to be fixed.

Do you remember?

A singular noun names one person, animal, thing, place, idea, or feeling.
These are singular nouns: **eel, loss, pot, wish**.
A plural noun names more than one.
These are plural nouns: **eels, losses, pots, wishes**.

Try it out.

Here are ten sentences. Check the naming words or nouns. Change any noun that is not correct. Write the correct nouns in the blanks.

1. I have had two rash this year.   _____

2. Last years Valerie lost ten pounds.   _____

3. Patti goes to two beach in the summer.   _____

4. We have three pass to the movies.   _____

5. Jesse wears an eye patches.   _____

6. There are ten witch in this movie.   _____

7. Be careful how you light those match.   _____

8. Scott has been in four car crash this year.   _____

9. Scott should not drive a cars.   _____

10. Louisa likes to ride in many bus.   _____

STOP CHECK ANSWERS ON PAGE 125.

THE WORD I (PRONOUN)

Read the following:

I do not want to meet Suzi.
I am tired.
Cathy and I can meet Suzi later.
Then Cathy, Suzi, and I can go to my house.

Did you notice?

The word **I** tells who is speaking.
A person uses **I** when he or she talks about himself or herself.
The word **I** comes last in a list of names.

Do you remember?

The words **he, she,** and **it** are used in place of naming words, or nouns.

Did you know?

The words **he, she, it,** and **I** are called **pronouns**.

Try it out.

Fill in each blank with **I**, **he**, **she**, or **it**.

1. Mino loves his new boat.

   _____ shows it to everyone.

2. My wife works three days a week.

   _____ sells makeup.

3. My wife loves to go for walks with me.

   _____ and _____ go for walks every night.

4. My boss wants me to work at night.

   _____ do not want to work at night.

5. This job does not pay very well.

   _____ is not a very good job.

STOP CHECK ANSWERS ON PAGE 125.

DESCRIBING WORDS (ADJECTIVES)

Read the following:

The silly child laughed and laughed.
My famous brother is visiting me now.

Did you notice?

The word **silly** describes the child.
The word **famous** describes the brother.

Do you remember?

Words like **silly** and **famous** are describing words.
Such words describe nouns, or naming words.
Words that describe nouns are called **adjectives**.

Try it out.

Write one adjective in each blank. Choose the **best** word to describe the naming word, or noun.

1. _____ banana (**tall, round, ripe**)

2. _____ fox (**salty, sly, low**)

3. _____ sponge (**short, silly, damp**)

4. _____ apple (**tired, short, juicy**)

5. _____ dress (**nice, ripe, sour**)

6. _____ candy (**dumb, soft, tall**)

7. _____ lemon (**red, heavy, sour**)

8. _____ sky (**heavy, blue, proud**)

9. _____ pillow (**dim, happy, fluffy**)

10. _____ grass (**safe, green, dim**)

STOP CHECK ANSWERS ON PAGE 125.

ACTION WORDS (VERBS)

Read the following:

The cat **drinks** milk.   The cats **drink** milk.
My boss **yells** a lot.   My bosses **yell** a lot.
John **works** hard.   John and Carol **work** hard.
Sharon **swims**.   Sharon, Sue, and I **swim**.

Do you remember?

Action words end with **s** when they tell about one person or one thing.

Try it out.

Write the correct action words, or verbs, in the blanks.

1. Kenneth and Sima (**works** or **work**) hard.   _____

2. Pasquale (**rides** or **ride**) well.   _____

3. The flowers (**blooms** or **bloom**) every year.   _____

4. My sisters (**sings** or **sing**) well.   _____

5. Maria (**drives** or **drive**) well.   _____

6. Samantha and I (**eats** or **eat**) good food.   _____

7. Cows (**moos** or **moo**).   _____

8. Tom and Mark (**plays** or **play**) ball on weekends.   _____

9. Louisa and José (**lives** or **live**) here.   _____

10. The child (**tastes** or **taste**) everything she bakes.   _____

STOP CHECK ANSWERS ON PAGE 125.

ACTION WORDS AND HELPING WORDS (VERBS)

Read the following:

I am running.   We are running.
Tony runs.   Tony and Willie run.
He is running.   He and I are running.
Carol runs.   Carol and Pauline run.
She is running.   They are running.
The bus runs.   The buses run.
It is running.   They are running.

Do you remember?

Action words, or verbs, end in **s** when they tell about one person or one thing.
The helping word **am** goes with **I**.
The helping word **is** goes with **he**, **she**, and **it**.
The helping word **are** goes with **we** and **they**.
The helping word **are** is also used when more than one person or thing do the action.

Try it out.

Choose the word or words that complete each sentence correctly. Circle the correct verbs.

1. It (**is raining** or **are raining**) hard today.

2. My brother and I (**likes** or **like**) to eat hot dogs.

3. He (**is driving** or **are driving**) a bus now.

4. Tony (**writes** or **write**) well.

5. My wife (**shares** or **share**) everything with me.

6. We (**loves** or **love**) each other.

7. My brothers (**is helping** or **are helping**) us.

8. Jim, Dan, and I (**needs** or **need**) help.

9. That person (**is catching** or **are catching**) a lot of fish.

10. Charles (**earns** or **earn**) a good living.

STOP   CHECK ANSWERS ON PAGE 126.

ACTION WORDS (VERBS) NOW AND BEFORE NOW

Read the following:

Dave <u>plays</u> basketball.　　Those women <u>dress</u> well.
She <u>walks</u> a mile every day.　They <u>bake</u> good cakes.

Did you notice?

The sentences tell about actions that are usually repeated.

Now read the following:

Dave <u>played</u> basketball.　　The women <u>dressed</u> well.
She <u>walked</u> to work.　　　They <u>baked</u> good cakes.

Did you notice?

These sentences tell about actions that happened in the past, before now.

Did you know?

When a sentence tells about the past, the action word has a special ending. Most action words that describe the past end with **ed** or **d**.

USUALLY TAKES PLACE OR TAKES PLACE NOW	PAST, OR BEFORE NOW
I cook every day.	I cook**ed** that meal.
She works at night.	She work**ed** on the weekend.
He dances smoothly.	He danc**ed** in the contest.
They live nearby.	They once live**d** in Chicago.

Try it out.

Circle the correct verbs.

1. Yesterday I (**play** or **played**) football.

2. My son (**starts** or **started**) school the other day.

3. We now (**live** or **lived**) with my mother.

4. Ron (**works** or **worked**) hard at this time.

5. The other day our cat (**chases** or **chased**) a mouse through the house.

GO ON TO THE NEXT PAGE

6. It (**rains** or **rained**) before.

7. I (**like** or **liked**) to exercise in the morning now.

8. Cats (**wash** or **washed**) themselves all the time.

9. That dog (**barks** or **barked**) at me the last time I was here.

10. Miguel (**hates** or **hated**) rice now.

STOP CHECK ANSWERS ON PAGE 126.

WRITING A FRIENDLY LETTER

January 3, 1989 **date**

greeting *Dear Flo,*

body *My husband and I had a great time at your party. Thank you for inviting us.*

Your friend, **closing**
Diane **signature**

Did you notice?

At the top of the letter is the date: **June 3, 1989**.
The letter begins with a greeting: **Dear Flo,**.
The body of the letter contains the message.
The writer's letter ends with a closing and the writer's name: **Diane**.

Try it out.

Here is the form for a friendly letter. Write a thank-you letter to a friend.
Use today's date. End the letter with your name.

_____ , 19 ____

Dear _____ ,

_____

_____

_____

_____

Your friend,

_____

STOP CHECK SAMPLE LETTER ON PAGE 126.

THE ALPHABET

Read the following:

bar, ear, goose, air, fall, cane, drink

Now read the following:

air, bar, cane, drink, ear, fall, goose

Did you notice?

Only the second list is in the order of the alphabet.

Try it out.

Here are 26 words. Write them in alphabetical order.

work	job	home	zoo	rich	factory
child	bed	year	egg	x-ray	
ice	aunt	uncle	sister	game	
lamp	oven	name	king	queen	
dance	very	pet	mother	time	

A. _____   J. _____   S. _____

B. _____   K. _____   T. _____

C. _____   L. _____   U. _____

D. _____   M. _____   V. _____

E. _____   N. _____   W. _____

F. _____   O. _____   X. _____

G. _____   P. _____   Y. _____

H. _____   Q. _____   Z. _____

I. _____   R. _____

STOP CHECK ANSWERS ON PAGE 126.

CAPITAL LETTERS

Write the following sentences over. Use capital letters correctly.

1. mrs. janice garcia and i have been out of work since may.

2. on thursday i am meeting mr. heller to talk about a job.

3. miss fleishman says it is hard to find a new job.

4. mr. george harris was laid off on monday.

5. ms. donahue, mrs. hirsch, and i hope to find jobs by august.

TELLING AND ASKING SENTENCES

Write one word from this list in each blank in the sentences. Use each word only once. Add an end mark to each sentence. Be sure the completed sentences make sense.

WORD LIST

book	find	how	looking	mother
read	she	what	where	why

1. _____ many do you want

2. _____ have you done with my sweater

3. The _____ I am reading is very funny

4. Her _____ just lost her glasses

5. _____ can they be

6. Judy cannot _____ without her glasses

7. _____ keeps bumping into things

8. Everyone is _____ for the glasses

9. _____ can't they find them

10. No one can _____ them

GO ON TO THE NEXT PAGE

WORD ORDER IN SENTENCES

Use the following groups of words to write sentences. Put the words in correct order.

1. Lot Rebecca home a is alone.

_____

2. Children school in are her both.

_____

3. Find job Rebecca like to would a.

_____

4. Work husband want to does her her not.

_____

5. And bored to starting is Rebecca is much too drink.

_____

SENTENCE PARTS

Find the words from Group Two, the action part, that go with each naming part from Group One. Write the letter in the blank.

GROUP ONE (NAMING PART)

___ 1. Judy Randall

___ 2. Her husband Bryan

___ 3. They

___ 4. The baby

___ 5. The doctor

___ 6. The operation

___ 7. Their parents

___ 8. Bryan's boss

___ 9. The people at work

___ 10. They

GROUP TWO (ACTION PART)

a. had this baby right away.

b. do not have any money.

c. married at an early age.

d. was born with a heart problem.

e. is very costly.

f. want to raise thousands of dollars.

g. needs to operate on the child.

h. was also very young.

i. lets Bryan work overtime a lot.

j. are trying to raise money for the operation.

GO ON TO THE NEXT PAGE

NAMING WORDS (NOUNS)

Fill in each blank with a noun from this list. Use each word **only once**. Be sure the completed sentences make sense.

NOUN LIST

age	car	day	jobs	morning	night
pals	place	prison	school	store	time

1. Mike and I married at a very early _____ .

2. We both dropped out of _____ .

3. We had a hard _____ finding _____ .

4. We would be tired when we woke up in the _____ .

5. Often we would fight until late at _____ .

6. We lived in a terrible _____ .

7. One _____ Mike met some old _____ .

8. They talked him into robbing a _____ .

9. Mike drove the _____ .

10. Now I visit him in _____ .

MORE THAN ONE (PLURAL)

Change any naming word, or noun, that is not correct. Write the correct nouns in the blanks.

1. Elaine lit a matches.   _____

2. Nader belongs to two church.   _____

3. At work we have three boss.   _____

4. No one has a passes to the football game.   _____

5. I have seen two crash today.   _____

GO ON TO THE NEXT PAGE

THE WORD *I* (PRONOUN)

Fill in each blank with **I**, **he**, **she**, or **it**.

1. Artie likes to meet me for dinner.

   _____ and _____ have a good time.

2. Sharon enjoys sports.

   _____ goes to many ball games.

3. The rock hit a car.

   _____ hurt the driver.

4. My girlfriend doesn't like me to spend a lot of money.

   _____ is very careful with money.

5. The rain cleared the air.

   _____ also caused lots of floods.

RECOGNIZING DESCRIBING WORDS (ADJECTIVES)

Draw lines under all the words that describe naming words.

1. My famous father writes good stories and books.

2. He writes short, scary stories.

3. There are many gory murders in his stories.

4. I don't read his frightening tales on dark, rainy nights.

5. He is a good storyteller.

ACTION WORDS (VERBS)

Write the correct action words, or verbs, in the blanks.

1. James (**smokes** or **smoke**) too much.   _____

2. The birds (**sings** or **sing**) too loud.   _____

3. Margaret (**draws** or **draw**) well.   _____

4. Abdul and Razzia (**travels** or **travel**) a lot.   _____

5. I (**hates** or **hate**) travelling.   _____

GO ON TO THE NEXT PAGE

6. Jack (**loves** or **love**) to fly.   _____

7. His brother (**fears** or **fear**) flying.   _____

8. I (**likes** or **like**) to stay home.   _____

9. My dog (**enjoys** or **enjoy**) our house. _____

10. My cat (**sleeps** or **sleep**) inside.   _____

ACTION WORDS AND HELPING WORDS (VERBS)

Choose the word or words that complete each sentence correctly. Circle the correct verbs.

1. The man (**is running** or **are running**) fast.

2. Two police officers (**is chasing** or **are chasing**) him.

3. It (**is snowing** or **are snowing**).

4. The ground (**is** or **are**) slippery.

5. The robber (**slips** or **slip**) on the ice.

6. The police officers (**slips** or **slip**) on the ice.

7. They (**is** or **are**) all on the ground.

8. It (**is** or **are**) a funny sight.

9. A police officer (**puts** or **put**) handcuffs on the robber.

10. Crime (**does** or **do**) not pay.

ACTION WORDS (VERBS) NOW AND BEFORE NOW

Circle each correct action word, or verb.

1. Mrs. Johnson (**phones** or **phoned**) just before.

2. She (**helps** or **helped**) me yesterday.

3. I (**need** or **needed**) her a lot now.

4. Jamie (**stops** or **stopped**) me from hurting myself yesterday.

5. The flowers (**look** or **looked**) lovely this year.

GO ON TO THE NEXT PAGE

WRITING A FRIENDLY LETTER

Write a letter to someone thanking him or her for inviting you to dinner. Use today's date. End the letter with your name.

_____ , 19 _____

Dear _____ ,

_____

_____

_____

_____

Your friend,

_____

THE ALPHABET

Write these 26 words in alphabetical order. Put commas between the words you write.

fat, Antonia, name, José, Dan, x-ray, Linda, run, Sally, yell
Betty, get, iron, can, open, queen, kill, us, zoo, eleven, vase
home, Mohammed, Peter, Tran, wet,

_____

_____

_____

_____

_____

STOP CHECK ANSWERS BEGINNING ON PAGE 126.

Count how many items you answered correctly in each **Section** of the Chapter Four Review. Write your score per section in the **My Scores** column. If all of your section scores are as high as the **Good Scores,** go on to Chapter Five. If any of your section scores are lower than the **Good Scores,** study the lessons on the assigned **Review Pages** again before you go on to Chapter Five.

Section	Good Scores	My Scores	Review Pages
Capital Letters	4 or 5		64
Telling and Asking Sentences	8, 9, or 10		65–66
Word Order in Sentences	4 or 5		67
Sentence Parts	8, 9, or 10		68
Naming Words (Nouns)	8, 9, or 10		70
More Than One (Plural)	4 or 5		71
The Word **I** (Pronoun)	4 or 5		72
Recognizing Describing Words (Adjectives)	4 or 5		73
Action Words (Verbs)	8, 9, or 10		74
Action Words and Helping Words (Verbs)	8, 9, or 10		75
Action Words (Verbs) Now and Before Now	4 or 5		76–77
Writing a Friendly Letter	A correct letter		78
The Alphabet	All correct		79

CHAPTER FIVE

CAPITAL LETTERS

Read the following:

Mr. D. Beranski and Ms. S. Loveland are here.
Miss Maria M. Veldez will attend the meeting.
Mr. and Mrs. James J. Kennedy will not attend.

Did you notice?

The initials **D.**, **S.**, **M.**, and **J.** are capital letters.
Those initials are the first letters of names.
They are used in place of names.
There is a period (.) after each initial.

Do you remember?

People's names and titles begin with capital letters.
The word **I** is written with a capital letter.
Every sentence begins with a capital letter.
The names of the days and months begin with capital letters.

Try it out.

Write the following sentences over. Use capital letters correctly.

1. mr. and mrs. j. d. bank and i like to bowl.

   _____

2. miss r. s. silver does not like her boss, mr. fred j. gray.

   _____

3. did ms. mary r. stavos write that to mrs. m. m. garrison last month?

   _____

4. who are m. m. worth and s. f. cortez?

   _____

5. i think k. m. blue and henry i. singer are crooks.

   _____

GO ON TO THE NEXT PAGE

6. mrs. peggy m. johns read that jim r. white won the lottery.

_____

7. i do not know how much mr. j. r. white won in december.

_____

8. mr. and mrs. john f. tabrizi and their son jeff need help.

_____

9. jeff tabrizi ran away from home last monday.

_____

10. his parents and a friend, mrs. j. j. rose, found him on tuesday.

_____

STOP CHECK ANSWERS ON PAGE 127.

WRITING TELLING AND ASKING SENTENCES

Try it out.

Here are five pairs of words. First, write a telling sentence using the words. Then write an asking sentence using the same words.

1. pet   needs

   _____

   _____

2. company   is

   _____

   _____

3. car   does

   _____

   _____

4. I   cook

   _____

   _____

5. people   like

   _____

   _____

STOP CHECK SAMPLE ANSWERS ON PAGE 128.

WORD ORDER IN SENTENCES

Read the following:

Work Janice going today is to?

Did you notice?

The words do not mean anything.
They do not make a sentence.
They should say this:

Is Janice going to work today?

Do you remember?

The words must be in correct order for a sentence to make sense.

Try it out.

Use the following groups of words to write questions. Put the words in correct order.

1. Leaving why you work are early so?

_____

2. Stephen lose did today the race?

_____

3. Pay new for suit how did much you your?

_____

4. Saw who house her you into going?

_____

5. Trouble always boss with in you are the why?

_____

STOP CHECK ANSWERS ON PAGE 128.

SENTENCE PARTS

Read the following:

The goat chews.	The goats chew.
Carol dresses well.	Carol and Sharon dress well.
The boy fishes.	The boys fish.
Pedro pitches.	Pedro and Mike pitch.

Did you notice?

When a noun names one person, thing, or animal, the verb ends with **s** or **es**.

The **es** ending is used with verbs that end with **ss**, **sh**, or **ch**, like **dress**, **fish**, and **pitch**.

Try it out.

Find the words from Group Two, the action part, that go with each naming part from Group One. Write the letter in the blank.

GROUP ONE (NAMING PART)	GROUP TWO (ACTION PART)
____ 1. The janitor	**a.** needs a coat of paint.
____ 2. These pears	**b.** hatch eggs.
____ 3. Those artists	**c.** catch the fly balls.
____ 4. My mother	**d.** taste good.
____ 5. His house	**e.** takes care of the building.
____ 6. Those players	**f.** loves her children.
____ 7. Hens	**g.** live together.
____ 8. The police	**h.** paint well.
____ 9. Carl and Angela	**i.** runs the factory.
____ 10. My boss	**j.** are searching for the robbers.

STOP CHECK ANSWERS ON PAGE 128.

WRITING SENTENCES

Read the following:

I work _____ for my _____ .
They _____ many _____ .
One of these words belongs in each blank in the sentences above:
family   hard   need   things

Did you notice?

The sentences should be completed this way:
I work <u>hard</u> for my <u>family</u>.
They <u>need</u> many <u>things</u>.

Try it out.

Fill in each blank with a word from this list. Use each word **only once**. Be sure the completed sentences make sense.

WORD LIST

best	date	go	is	older
pretty	school	sister	working	young

1. My _____ friend _____ getting married.

2. He used to _____ my _____ sister.

3. My sister is still in _____ and is too _____ to get married.

4. My friend is _____ and is much _____ than she.

5. My _____ refuses to _____ to my friend's wedding.

STOP CHECK ANSWERS ON PAGE 128.

NAMING WORDS (NOUNS)

Do you remember?

Naming words are words such as the following:
   lady, man, child, girl, food, flower, picture, ape, peanut, sink, job, home, town.
Naming words are nouns.
They name persons, animals, things, places, ideas, or feelings.

Try it out.

Fill in each blank with a noun from this list. Use each word **only once**. Be sure the completed sentences make sense.

NOUN LIST

boyfriend	brother	children	family	friend
man	school	secrets	sister	years

1. My best _____ Alice is getting married soon.

2. I have known her for twenty _____.

3. We went to grade _____ together.

4. I am married to her _____ Robert.

5. Alice is like a _____ to me.

6. I tell her all my _____.

7. Alice wants to have four _____.

8. She comes from a large _____.

9. Her _____ is a truck driver.

10. He is a well-built _____.

STOP CHECK ANSWERS ON PAGE 128.

MORE THAN ONE (PLURAL)

Read the following:

I have only one trunks.
It is several years old.
Both latch on the trunk are broken.

Did you notice?

Nouns in the first and last sentences are wrong.
The correct sentences are these:
I have only one **trunk**.
Both **latches** on the trunk are broken.

Do you remember?

Many plural nouns end with **s** or **es**.
The **es** ending follows **ch**, **s**, **sh**, and **ss**: notches, buses, dishes, masses.

Try it out.

Check the naming words, or nouns, in these sentences. Change any noun that is not correct. If the sentence is correct, put a **C** in the blank.

1. Nine year is a long time to wait. _____

2. I have both watch. _____

3. Here is a ripe peaches. _____

4. I made one batches of cookies. _____

5. My three sister are pretty. _____

6. Seth gave several speech. _____

7. There are four church in our town. _____

8. We have many tennis match here. _____

9. Do you have a match? _____

10. Who is baking the six pie? _____

STOP CHECK ANSWERS ON PAGE 128.

THE WORD *THEY* (PRONOUN)

Read the following:

Marcella and Carmen live near each other.
They drive to work together.
My mother and father are happy that I have a job.
They are proud of me.
The workers didn't like the way they were treated.
They went on strike.

Did you notice?

The word **they** is used in place of naming words.
The word **they** refers to more than one person, animal, place, thing, idea, or feeling.

Try it out.

Fill in the blank in each sentence with **he, she, it, I,** or **they**.

1. The men were late for work.

   _____ had stopped to eat breakfast.

2. Mr. Rizzoli was not angry.

   _____ is an understanding boss.

3. Jill isn't at work today.

   _____ is ill.

4. My boss told me to stay home today.

   _____ like him a lot.

5. Michael and Robert are leaving work early.

   _____ are going to a ball game.

6. Mrs. Simpson is her boss.

   _____ has been here for years.

GO ON TO THE NEXT PAGE

7. The young people don't stay long.

   _____ leave in a few months.

8. This job is hard.

   _____ does not pay well.

9. My girlfriend wants me to quit.

   _____ and _____ talk about quitting a lot.

10. My friends are also talking about quitting.

    _____ think they can get better jobs.

STOP CHECK ANSWERS ON PAGE 128.

DESCRIBING WORDS (ADJECTIVES)

Read the following:

The handsome guy smiles at everyone.
The shy fellow does not talk much.

Did you notice?

The word **handsome** tells about the guy.
The word **shy** tells about the fellow.

Do you remember?

Words like **handsome** and **shy** are describing words.
Such words describe nouns, or naming words.
They are called **adjectives**.

Try it out.

Fill in each blank with an adjective from the list. Choose the **best** word to describe the naming word, or noun.

ADJECTIVE LIST

cold	correct	handsome	noisy	pretty
sharp	soft	stubborn	swift	tame

1. _____ water

2. _____ woman

3. _____ man

4. _____ animal

5. _____ deer

6. _____ knife

7. _____ cloth

8. _____ mule

9. _____ party

10. _____ word

STOP   CHECK ANSWERS ON PAGE 128.

ACTION WORDS (VERBS)

Read the following:

José <u>works</u> at my school.   Sue and José <u>work</u> at my school.
Cary <u>rushes</u> to work every day.   They <u>rush</u> to leave at night.
Jim <u>bosses</u> everyone a lot.   They <u>boss</u> everyone a lot.
Hank <u>catches</u> colds often.   Sally and Hank <u>catch</u> colds often.

Do you remember?

Action words end with **s** or **es** when they tell about one person or one thing.

Try it out.

Write the correct action words, or verbs, in the blanks.

1. Keung (**swims** or **swim**).   _____

2. The pitcher (**catches** or **catch**).   _____

3. Jerry (**rushes** or **rush**) home.   _____

4. Dogs and wolves (**growls** or **growl**).   _____

5. The dancers (**jumps** or **jump**).   _____

6. The men (**works** or **work**) hard.   _____

7. Harry and Martha (**helps** or **help**)
   Miguel.   _____

8. Eleni (**teaches** or **teach**) typing.   _____

9. The minister (**preaches** or **preach**)
   every week.   _____

10. Full buckets (**splashes** or **splash**).   _____

STOP CHECK ANSWERS ON PAGE 128.

ACTION WORDS AND HELPING WORDS (VERBS)

Read the following:

I work.	Jack and I work.
I am working.	Jack and I are working.
He works.	They work.
He is working.	They are working.
The stove works.	The stoves work.
The stove is working.	The stoves are working.

Do you remember?

The helping word **am** goes with **I**.
The helping verb **is** goes with one person or thing.
The helping verb **are** goes with more than one person or thing.

Try it out.

Choose the word that completes each sentence correctly. Circle each correct verb.

1. He (**is** or **are**) a happy person.

2. The boys (**fishes** or **fish**) every day.

3. The youngsters (**laughs** or **laugh**) a lot.

4. Swimming and dancing (**is** or **are**) fun.

5. I (**loves** or **love**) to bowl.

6. My girlfriend (**spends** or **spend**) too much money.

7. Thomas and Margaret (**fights** or **fight**) a lot.

8. Sara, Lisa, and Claude (**is** or **are**) friends.

9. The firefighters (**is** or **are**) here.

10. It (**is** or **are**) not fair to do that.

STOP CHECK ANSWERS ON PAGE 128.

ACTION WORDS (VERBS) NOW AND BEFORE NOW

Try it out.

Rewrite each sentence so that it shows past time.

1. My sister plays the drums.   _____

2. My friends park at the station.   _____

3. Clara waits for me.   _____

4. Ben, José, and I miss you.   _____

5. We live in three rooms.   _____

6. He shows us new things.   _____

7. Pedro races cars.   _____

8. Sally dines alone.   _____

9. He fails all his tests.   _____

10. Noriko and I sail a large boat.   _____

STOP CHECK ANSWERS ON PAGE 128.

WRITING A FRIENDLY LETTER

Do you remember?

The date goes at the top of a letter.
A greeting begins a letter.
The body gives the message.
A closing and signature end a letter.

Try it out.

Here is the form for a friendly letter. You are away on a trip. Write a letter to a friend describing the trip. Use today's date. End the letter with your name.

————————— , 19 ———

Dear ——————— ,

———————————————————

———————————————————

———————————————————

———————————————————

Your friend,

———————————

STOP CHECK SAMPLE LETTER ON PAGE 129.

THE ALPHABET

Read the following:

cross   favor   axe   escort   date   bottom

Now read the following:

axe   bottom   cross   date   escort   favor

Did you notice?

Only the second list is in the order of the alphabet.

Try it out.

Here are 26 words. Write them in alphabetical order.

butter   rain   x-ray   old   write   sign   fear   ant   land   dark   year
jam   very   quick   hand   use   grade   zebra   name   park   tent   map
egg   Indian   candy   kite

A. _____   J. _____   S. _____

B. _____   K. _____   T. _____

C. _____   L. _____   U. _____

D. _____   M. _____   V. _____

E. _____   N. _____   W. _____

F. _____   O. _____   X. _____

G. _____   P. _____   Y. _____

H. _____   Q. _____   Z. _____

I. _____   R. _____

STOP   CHECK ANSWERS ON PAGE 129.

CAPITAL LETTERS

Write the following sentences over. Use capital letters correctly.

1. mr. and mrs. h. j. washington won the lottery in june.

2. their son robert w. washington keeps giving parties.

3. ms. r. s. chan is their banker.

4. she and mr. james t. travis want the washingtons to save their money.

5. their daughter betty ann is leaving thursday for a trip around the world.

TELLING AND ASKING SENTENCES

Here are five pairs of words.
First write a telling sentence using the words.
Then write an asking sentence using the same words.

1. I   work

_____

_____

2. boss   help

_____

_____

3. players   refuse

_____

_____

4. brother   buys

_____

_____

GO ON TO THE NEXT PAGE

5. house   needs

_____

_____

WORD ORDER IN SENTENCES

Use the following groups of words to write sentences. Put the words in correct order.

1. In love Felipe boss is his with.

_____

2. Woman boss a his is.

_____

3. Boss good she a is.

_____

4. Thinks Felipe all about the her time.

_____

5. Mind get he her out his of cannot.

_____

WRITING SENTENCES

Fill in each blank with a word from this list. Use each word **only once**. Be sure the completed sentences make sense.

WORD LIST

husband	I	is	know	parent
school	son	wants	work	years

1. I am a single _____ .

2. My _____ left me ten _____ ago.

3. I do not _____ where he _____ .

4. My _____ and _____ work hard.

5. He _____ to leave _____ and go to

_____ .

GO ON TO THE NEXT PAGE

NAMING WORDS (NOUNS)

Fill in each blank with a noun from this list. Use each word **only once**. Be sure the completed sentences make sense.

NOUN LIST

arms	bedroom	boys	cat	dog
food	legs		man	paint	shave

1. My _____ needs a coat of _____ .

2. That _____ needs a _____ .

3. The barking _____ found his bowl of _____ .

4. My _____ and _____ hurt from exercise.

5. Those _____ hurt the _____ .

MORE THAN ONE (PLURAL)

Check the naming words, or nouns, in these sentences. Change any noun that is not correct. Write the correct nouns in the blanks.

1. Do you have three watch? _____

2. The player made a great catches. _____

3. I have one bosses who talks a lot. _____

4. The two princess in the story are very beautiful. _____

5. Brian wash the car every day. _____

THE WORD *THEY* (PRONOUN)

Fill in each blank with **he**, **she**, **it**, **I**, or **they**.

1. Roberto and Dave build houses together.

   _____ have been doing this for a long time.

2. The houses are well built.

   _____ cost a lot.

3. Roberto wants to build a house for himself.

   _____ doesn't have the time.

GO ON TO THE NEXT PAGE

4. His wife is angry with him.

_____ wants a new house.

5. His work keeps him away from his home a lot.

_____ is causing a strain on their marriage.

RECOGNIZING DESCRIBING WORDS (ADJECTIVES)

Draw a line under all the words that describe naming words.

1. The new leader tried to cheer his tired men.

2. The dirty, tired men needed good, hot meals.

3. They had been marching for many days.

4. They wanted to get rid of their heavy packs.

5. The cool, dry night calmed the weary soldiers.

ACTION WORDS (VERBS)

Write the correct action words, or verbs, in the blanks.

1. Betsy (**starts** or **start**) drinking in the morning. _____

2. She (**drinks** or **drink**) until the evening. _____

3. She (**eats** or **eat**) nothing all day. _____

4. She (**cooks** or **cook**) nothing. _____

5. Betsy (**hides** or **hide**) her drinking from everyone. _____

6. She (**does** or **do**) not clean the house. _____

7. Betsy (**stays** or **stay**) home all the time. _____

8. Few friends (**calls** or **call**) her. _____

9. People (**scares** or **scare**) Betsy. _____

10. They (**sees** or **see**) something is wrong. _____

GO ON TO THE NEXT PAGE

ACTION WORDS AND HELPING WORDS (VERBS)

Circle the verb that completes each sentence correctly.

1. The poor homeless man (**is** or **are**) begging.

2. Many homeless people (**needs** or **need**) help.

3. They (**is** or **are**) roaming the streets.

4. It (**is** or **are**) becoming dangerous to live on the street.

5. A person (**is** or **are**) not safe.

ACTION WORDS (VERBS) NOW AND BEFORE NOW

Write the following verbs over to show past time.

1. jump _____   6. cook _____

2. play _____   7. clean _____

3. work _____   8. start _____

4. dream _____   9. help _____

5. camp _____   10. dance _____

GO ON TO THE NEXT PAGE

WRITING A FRIENDLY LETTER

You are on a trip. Write a letter to someone describing your trip.

_____ , 19 ____

Dear _____ ,

_____

_____

_____

_____

_____

Your friend,

_____

THE ALPHABET

Write these words in alphabetical order. Put commas between the words in the list you write.

Cathy, Edward, Maria, Pedro, David, Ira, Rita, George, Linda, Neda, Oliver, Henry, Sachiko, Juan, Ann, Karl, Tom, Bijan, Franco, Verva

_____

_____

_____

_____

_____

STOP CHECK ANSWERS BEGINNING ON PAGE 129.

Count how many items you answered correctly in each **Section** of the Chapter Five Review. Write your score per section in the **My Scores** column. If all of your section scores are as high as the **Good Scores,** take the Posttest. If any of your section scores are lower than the **Good Scores,** study the lessons on the assigned **Review Pages** again before you take the Posttest.

Section	Good Scores	My Scores	Review Pages
Capital Letters	4 or 5		88–89
Telling and Asking Sentences	4 or 5		90
Word Order in Sentences	4 or 5		91
Writing Sentences	4 or 5		93
Naming Words (Nouns)	4 or 5		94
More Than One (Plural)	4 or 5		95
The Word **They** (Pronoun)	4 or 5		96–97
Recognizing Describing Words (Adjectives)	4 or 5		98
Action Words (Verbs)	8, 9, or 10		99
Action Words and Helping Words (Verbs)	4 or 5		100
Action Words (Verbs) Now and Before Now	8, 9, or 10		101
Writing a Friendly Letter	A correct letter		102
The Alphabet	All correct		103

CAPITAL LETTERS

Write the following sentences over. Use capital letters correctly.

1. miss martha m. kendall and mr. josé s. torres are getting married.

_____

2. the wedding will be on a sunday in june.

_____

3. the bride's parents, mr. and mrs. a. r. kendall, are very happy.

_____

4. the groom's parents, mr. and mrs. r. s. torres, are also happy.

_____

5. helen, sharon, hector, and i are in the wedding party.

_____

TELLING AND ASKING SENTENCES

Write the following sentences over. Use correct capital letters and end marks.

1. fred and i are going into business together

_____

2. he is good with his hands

_____

3. i will be the brains of the business

_____

4. do you think we are a good team

_____

5. who will put up the money for us to start

_____

GO ON TO THE NEXT PAGE

WORD ORDER IN SENTENCES

Write the following groups of words over. Write sentences that make sense. Put the words in correct order.

1. Woman grabbed the from the robber pocketbook the.

   _____

2. Robber woman after the ran the.

   _____

3. Help for screamed woman the.

   _____

4. Think you her people do helped?

   _____

5. Tripped foot his robber the man a stuck and out.

   _____

NAMING WORDS (NOUNS)

Fill in each blank with a noun from this list. Use each noun **only once**. Be sure the completed sentences make sense.

NOUN LIST

car	chance	day	ears	friend
people	problem	shower	singer	truth

This may sound silly, but I always wanted to be a _____ .
                                                        (1)

I would sing while taking a _____ . I would sing in my
                              (2)

_____ . Whenever I had a _____ , I would sing.
   (3)   (4)

The _____ was nobody could stand my singing. One
      (5)

_____ my best _____ told me the
   (6)   (7)

_____ about my singing. He told me I did not sing well. Most
   (8)

_____ held their _____ when I sang.
   (9)   (10)

GO ON TO THE NEXT PAGE

RECOGNIZING NAMING WORDS (NOUNS)

Draw a line under each naming word, or noun, in the following sentences.

1. My family loves holidays.
2. On a holiday my aunts, uncles, and cousins visit my family.
3. One aunt always bakes good rolls and bread.
4. Another aunt brings cookies and cakes.
5. My cousins and I play softball and basketball all day.

MORE THAN ONE (PLURAL)

Rewrite any naming word, or noun, that is not correct. Put a **C** in the blank if the naming word is correct.

1. ten hose	_____	6. both pass	_____
2. some wish	_____	7. six grape	_____
3. several book	_____	8. one desks	_____
4. two ranch	_____	9. many irons	_____
5. a dreams	_____	10. three wash	_____

RECOGNIZING ACTION WORDS (VERBS)

Draw a line under the action word, or verb, in each sentence.

1. The lost child cried.
2. A police officer asked the child his name.
3. The child showed bruises on his arms and legs.
4. The police officer noticed the marks on the child.
5. She took the child to a hospital.

ACTION WORDS (VERBS)

Circle the verb that completes each sentence correctly.

1. Francis and I (**drives** or **drive**) too fast.
2. Billy always (**gets** or **get**) us into trouble.

GO ON TO THE NEXT PAGE

3. James (**throws** or **throw**) the ball too hard.

4. Wanda (**dresses** or **dress**) nicely.

5. Her sister (**tells** or **tell**) good stories.

ACTION WORDS (VERBS) NOW AND BEFORE NOW

Circle each correct action word, or verb.

1. Robert and I (**help** or **helped**) them earlier.

2. My boss still (**bowls** or **bowled**) every Monday after work.

3. My wife (**works** or **worked**) hard yesterday.

4. Sara (**refuses** or **refused**) to go there last time.

5. That police officer (**likes** or **liked**) us now.

THE WORDS *AM, ARE,* AND *IS*

Fill in each blank with **am**, **are**, or **is**.

1. She _____ always happy.

2. They _____ not friends.

3. _____ you her sister?

4. _____ she your cousin?

5. I _____ not her sister.

ACTION WORDS AND HELPING WORDS (VERBS)

Fill in each blank with **am**, **are**, or **is**.

1. They _____ staying for dinner.

2. Alan and I _____ going away.

3. My friend _____ working late today.

4. _____ they voting for him?

5. _____ I going too fast for you?

GO ON TO THE NEXT PAGE

THE WORDS HE, SHE, IT, I, AND THEY

Fill in each blank with **he**, **she**, **it**, **I**, or **they**.

1. My dog ran away yesterday.

   _____ is lost.

2. Theodore left the gate door open.

   _____ feels sorry about that.

3. My friend Seth helped me look for my dog.

   _____ and _____ had no luck.

4. My girlfriend misses my dog.

   _____ is looking, too.

5. My parents are upset about this.

   _____ like my dog a lot.

RECOGNIZING DESCRIBING WORDS (ADJECTIVES)

Draw a line under every word that describes a naming word.

1. The mean old witch carried a crooked stick.

2. The poor, tired old man looked at the pretty flowers.

3. The young boy and girl walked on the soft green grass.

4. My pretty, new red coat has a little black collar.

5. I like to wear my old blue jeans and large white shirt.

THE WORDS A AND AN

Write **a** or **an** in front of the following words.

1. _____ ape   6. _____ person

2. _____ iron   7. _____ woman

3. _____ earring   8. _____ pet

4. _____ ant   9. _____ ocean

5. _____ onion   10. _____ island

GO ON TO THE NEXT PAGE

WRITING A FRIENDLY LETTER

Write a friendly letter to someone. Thank him or her for taking you out for dinner. Use today's date. End the letter with your name.

_____, 19 ____

Dear _____,

_____

_____

_____

Your friend,

_____

THE ALPHABET

Write these 26 words in alphabetical order.

dark	zero	map	aunt	run	big	year	kill	call
eagle	has	was	one	x-ray	sew	fat	use	iron
now	jar	land	park	two	quick	girl	very	

1. _____   10. _____   19. _____

2. _____   11. _____   20. _____

3. _____   12. _____   21. _____

4. _____   13. _____   22. _____

5. _____   14. _____   23. _____

6. _____   15. _____   24. _____

7. _____   16. _____   25. _____

8. _____   17. _____   26. _____

9. _____   18. _____

STOP CHECK ANSWERS BEGINNING ON PAGE 130.

116

Count how many items you answered correctly in each **Section** of the Posttest. Write your score per section in the **My Scores** column. If all of your section scores are as high as the **Good Scores,** go on to *Power English 2,* Chapter One. If any of your section scores are lower than the **Good Scores,** study the lessons on the assigned **Review Pages** again before you go to *Power English 2,* Chapter One.

Section	Good Scores	My Scores	Review Pages
Capital Letters	4 or 5		2–3, 22–23, 42, 64, 88–89
Telling and Asking Sentences	4 or 5		4–6, 24–26, 43, 65–66, 90
Word Order in Sentences	4 or 5		28–29, 44, 67, 91
Naming Words (Nouns)	8, 9, or 10		8, 30, 45, 70, 94
Recognizing Naming Words (Nouns)	4 or 5		9, 31, 46
More Than One (Plural)	8, 9, or 10		10–11, 32–33, 47, 71, 95
Recognizing Action Words (Verbs)	4 or 5		13, 35
Action Words (Verbs)	4 or 5		12, 34, 54, 74, 99
Action Words (Verbs) Now and Before Now	4 or 5		76–77, 101
The Words **Am, Are,** and **Is**	4 or 5		52–53
Action Words and Helping Words (Verbs)	4 or 5		55, 75, 100

Section	Good Scores	My Scores	Review Pages
The Words **He, She, It, I,** and **They**	4 or 5		48–49, 72, 96–97
Recognizing Describing Words (Adjectives)	4 or 5		50–51, 73, 98
The Words **A** and **An**	8, 9, or 10		14
Writing a Friendly Letter	A correct letter		78, 102
The Alphabet	All correct		15–16, 36, 56, 79, 103